BREAKING CHAINS

The 6 Links of Turning Bondage into Tools of Freedom

2nd Edition

BLAKE B. SHELLEY

WHAT OTHERS ARE SAYING ABOUT BLAKE B. SHELLEY, HIS MISSION, BOOKS & SPEAKING

"In my life, I have overcome many obstacles and broken just as many chains, this book helps to put you on the path to overcoming whatever life throws at you. Blake takes a complicated concept and makes it accessible and less daunting."

—**Josh Blue**, comedian & winner of NBC's
Last Comic Standing

"The disability community uses the phrase 'Nothing about us without us' to say that in order to understand disability, you need to see and hear the experience through the life of a person with a disability. Blake's book will teach you about living fully and proudly with cerebral palsy. But Blake's writing is truly universal. His book teaches us about persistence, innovation, overcoming adversity and what it looks like to pursue your wildest dreams."

—**Dan Habib,** creator of the film *Including Samuel,*
about his son Samuel, who also experiences cerebral palsy.

"Writing a book can be a daunting challenge for anyone, but as a person with a disability, it can be even more so. I'm glad to know you and I share the same motto: Don't Take No For An Answer."

—**Steve Harrison,** Expert Publicly Consultant
& Co-Creator of the Bestseller Blueprint with Jack Canfield

"Blake reveals the true essence of the human spirit and provides inspiration to anyone looking to go beyond mediocrity and find their voice and passion. Breaking Chains will certainly motivate you to live the life worth living!"

—**Christopher Cumby,** Author of *The Success Playbook*
& Host of Think Bold, Be Bold podcast

"Breaking Chains is an amazingly written book about reaching your fullest potential. Many of us are like oak trees in a flowerpot, and we are root-bound by our own inhibitions. However, Blake has laid out a framework for how to overcome life's trials and tribulations to be the best you can be. This book is relevant to everyone!"

—**Ed Allen,** President
WCP Solutions

"'Why Not, I know I can' are often our responses as kids as we face opportunity or challenge; we tether no bias and harbor no trepidation. As we grow though, we become callous to change and retreat to grounds of comfort and illusinary safety, and there we remain as our chains hold us from what was once possible as children. Blake embodies the 'Why not, I know I can' practice of looking at life's hurdles and opportunity, as he has overcome so many. Blake will enlighten your soul and fill your tool box as he guides you along the road to escaping your bondage, whatever it may be. Blake is indeed an 'Angel on Earth'; reach out to him and be amazed; Connect and Rejoice"

—**Allan Wich,** Author of *The Change 6*
& Co-Host of Think Bold, Be Bold podcast

"Blake inspires students to reach their full potential through his personal testimony but also through classroom lessons on treating yourself and others with respect. He reaches students with his genuine care and kindness and encourages them to recognize opportunities to be helpful, supportive, and compassionate in the classroom, at home, and in their communities. Blake reminds kids and adults that a life with heart is a fulfilling life."

—**Elly Kendig,** 4th Grade Teacher
Portland Public School

"Blake is by far one of the most inspirational people I have ever met. He uses his disability to show others that anyone can overcome anything, as long as they work hard and have a good attitude about it."

—**Madison Adrian,** Undergraduate Student ('18),
Western Oregon University

"For the last three years I have been fortunate enough to have Blake Shelley present, mentor, and co-teach with me to my upper elementary classroom. Blake presents from a perspective that is often silenced in the general education classroom. He has taught my kids about perseverance, personal best, empathy, and thinking outside the box as to not be limited by the things that make you unique. He has not only touched my students but also the staff members in my building. Leading staff trainings and brainstorming with teachers about how to meet student needs are only the beginning of what he has to offer. I feel so fortunate to have him as a partner in teaching the generation of the future."

—**Katherine Wich,** 5th Grade Teacher
Portland Public Schools

"Blake Shelley has been a good friend of mine for multiple years now. Last year he came and spoke to my exceptional learners class. As someone who has a passion for special education and the uniqueness of the individual, this was an unforgettable experience. Blake embodies someone who is up for anything, and this showed in his presentation to my class. This presentation changed perspectives for many students, and I believe Blake will continue to change the lives of the many people he comes in contact with."

—**Bailey Newell,** Undergraduate Student ('17)

Warner Pacific College

MOTIVATE, INSPIRE AND EMPOWER OTHERS!
"Share This Book"

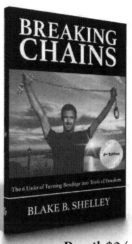

Retail $24.95

Special Quantity Discounts (Hardcover)

5-20 Books	$21.95
21-99 Books	$18.95
100-499 Books	$15.95
500-999 Books	$10.95
1,000+ Books	$8.95

To Place an Order, Contact:
(347) 690-5154
info@BlakeShelley.com
www.BlakeShelley.com
www.BreakingChainsBooks.com

THE IDEAL PROFESSIONAL SPEAKER FOR YOUR NEXT EVENT!

Any organization that wants to empower their people to become resilient, needs to hire Blake for a keynote and/or workshop training!

TO CONTACT OR BOOK BLAKE TO SPEAK:

Blake B. Shelley International
P.O. Box 195
Fairview, OR 97024

(347) 690-5154
info@BlakeShelley.com
www.BlakeShelley.com
www.BreakingChainsBooks.com

DEDICATION

To my mom, my dad, Brooke, and Rebecca, thank you for instilling in me an attitude of perseverance, showing me unconditional love, and always encouraging me to dream big!

I'd also like to dedicate this book to the Wich family and Allen Family, as they continue to be a constant source of support and encouragement!

Companion Resources

To enhance your experience with this book,
Blake has created *The Freedom Journal* and a *FREE* online course.

Get these resources at
www.BreakingChainsBooks.com

Table of Contents

Chapter 1: Introduction

IN THE LAST SEVERAL YEARS, I have been intrigued by the concept of chains. Throughout history, chains have been used for a variety of purposes, including as metaphors for the connections between events and entities. What do you think of when you hear about chains? Perhaps the use that comes to mind most frequently is that of keeping a prisoner in bondage. Others could say that it's a valuable tool used to support heavy objects. Both definitions are accurate; it's just how people choose to view them. As I reflect on chains, I can't help but draw parallels with the challenges and circumstances we face in our everyday lives. So often we feel bound, even paralyzed, by the challenges we face that we lose sight of our dreams. Could there be a healthier, more freeing way to view our challenges? Is it possible to take what once bound us and turn it into a tool that will help us reach our full potential? Not only do I believe it is possible, but I've lived it, and I know that you can too!

My name is Blake Shelley. I'm twenty-seven years old, and I am no stranger to the power of challenge and circumstance. I was born with Cerebral Palsy, which is a disability that affects my muscle movements and my fine motor skills. Since birth, I've had to persevere and overcome obstacles to accomplish things that come naturally to others. There have been many times where I have felt like a prisoner in my body and could have very easily given up. But living life as a prisoner—what fun would that be? What would I be contributing to my community if I sat in my room, isolated, not bettering myself, drooling, day after day? That would be such a waste of the precious gift of life! Even though I face challenges and pain on a daily basis, I choose to live life to the fullest extent. I set realistic goals, and I dream big! You can and should do the same!

Through my experience, I have subconsciously used a method that has helped me overcome and use my challenges to propel me toward my dreams. In today's culture of instant gratification, many people have lost sight of their goals and dreams. Unfortunately, we can't overcome challenges and reach our dreams as fast as we can order a movie or post a picture to Facebook. This process takes time and deep self-reflection. I'm writing this book to help you get from where you are to where you want to be.

Learn to Tell Your Story

Stories are the oldest form of communication and learning across all cultures. It is one thing we all have in common. However, everyone has a unique story. One of the most rewarding benefits of self-reflection is learning how to tell your story and identify the times in your life that shaped you into the person you are today. By learning to tell your story, both events of the past and what is happening in the present, you can find valuable lessons that will help you and others reach full potential.

Faith

Before we dive into how we turn our bondage into tools of freedom, I need to point out that this method requires a little faith. This can be faith in a deity, in yourself, in humanity, or a combination. In my case, my faith is rooted in my relationship with Jesus Christ. This relationship has given me the strength to rise above my circumstances and the belief that there are good-hearted people in this world.

Turning Bondage into Tools of Freedom

As I reflect on all of the challenges that I have conquered over my short life, I notice a common theme. This theme is one of self-reflection followed by setting a course of action. Striving to live life to the fullest, I have learned to run my challenges and circumstances through a process of reflection, which I refer to as the Six Links of Turning Bondage into Tools of Freedom. Through this process, I have been able to overcome my challenges just enough to use them as a tool and embrace the rest.

Let me paint a picture. Imagine that you are at the base of a mountain, longing to reach the summit. However, someone has put you in modern-day shackles, binding your hands and feet. You then realize that one of the links by your right hand is fragile and can be

easily removed. Now you have a free hand (with the cuff around it) and a few inches of strong chain to help pull you up the mountain.

This picture can be used to describe our quest to achieve our dreams. The following self-reflection exercise is to identify where you are, where you want to be, which links are easily removed, and which links you can use to pull yourself up.

The Six Links of Turning Bondage into Tools of Freedom

The Six Links of Turning Bondage into Tools of Freedom consists of What, Why, Where, When, How, and Who. Each of these links has several questions about your circumstance and your dreams. Don't worry if you can't answer them all at once. Remember, this is a process! However, by making a decision to enter into this process, you have taken a step toward freedom and success.

What

What is the challenge or circumstance holding me back? What are my chains?

_____

_____

What could this be teaching me?

_____

_____

Why

Why am I facing this challenge or circumstance?

_____

_____

Why do I feel that this situation is holding me back? Is it a physical, emotional, economical, or cultural challenge?

_____

_____

Where (In certain circumstances, it can be beneficial to identify where you want to be prior to defining your challenges.)

Where do I want to be? This is my dream.

_____

_____

When
When do I want to achieve this? Set goals and deadlines.

_____

_____

How

How am I going to reach this dream? Set small, practical goals.

_____

_____

How are these chains keeping me from taking steps toward this?

_____

_____

How can I remove some of these chains?

_____

_____

How can I take my current chains and use them to move forward?

_____

_____

How can I use previous experience(s) to help me move forward?

_____

_____

21

Who

With whom can I share the load? Who's in my corner?

_____

_____

Who is the ball on the end of this chain?

_____

_____

With whom can I link up? Find a mentor.

_____

_____

Whom can I help remove their chains of bondage?

_____

_____

Find a Support System

The sixth link has perhaps been the most influential in my life. Having a support system filled with people who genuinely care about our well-being and success is vital for us to rise up and reach the summit. We all need encouragement, someone in whom we can confide, someone to come alongside us, and someone to follow. Please don't go through life alone!

Come on a Journey

In the following chapters, I will recount how these links have radically changed my life and helped me reach my dreams. I invite you on this journey with me in hopes that you will also find the strength to turn your bondage into tools of freedom!

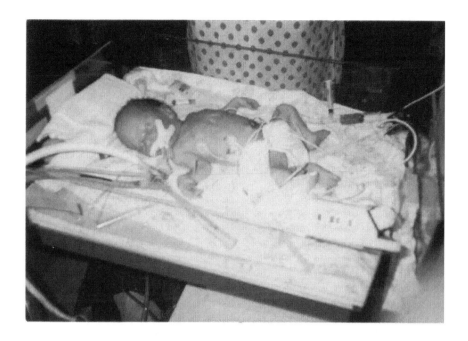

Chapter 2: Surviving

WHEN FACING OUR CHALLENGES FOR the first time, sometimes surviving is enough. Most of the challenges we face are triggered by a certain event or a chain of events over which we have little or no control. I like to think of this as the moment our shackles are slipped on and we're left at the base of the mountain in the cold. Although we often don't have control over events that create our adversities, we do have a say in how we respond. Every life-changing event presents us with a decision. Are we going to be paralyzed by our current situation or are we going to fight to survive?

My family and I were faced with this decision very early in my life. In fact, we encountered the event that altered our lives the morning I was born. Early one February morning my parents entered the hospital to bring life into the world. Little did they know what would transpire in the following hours and weeks to come.

The process of pregnancy is always a sensitive and miraculous time in one's life; my mom had carried twins a week past full term without any complications. A week prior to giving birth, my mom had an ultrasound to check if my sister and I were in the correct positions. At that time we were, but the doctor said that if anything changed they would have to perform a C-section.

However, as the birthing process began it was apparent that something was wrong. My sister had been born without complications and was being attended to by the nurses. Now it was my turn! Sometime between the last ultrasound and the beginning of labor, I had flipped, causing me to enter the canal "breech." Breech presentation is a term describing an infant who is either born legs first, or, in my case, leading with the buttocks. That's right, I started my life by mooning the doctor! Due to my position, it took over twenty minutes for me to enter the world, during many of which I was deprived of oxygen. As a result of this, I was presented blue and lifeless. As the doctors began CPR, my parents sat there in shock, praying that I would cry.

Once I was stable, I was transported to another hospital that had a neonatal ICU. Although I had survived the traumatic experience at birth, my future was still very unclear. Due to my brain injury, I proceeded to have multiple seizures throughout the first twenty-four hours. As the doctors updated my parents on the condition of their baby boy, they outlined several outcomes, including severe physical and mental disabilities or death. Because of this news and the trauma that she'd experienced, my mom was hesitant about seeing me for the first time. After talking with the nurses, she decided to come see me, and from then on I was rarely left alone! Over the course of my three-week hospital stay, I had a constant stream of visitors between my parents, grandparents, aunts, and uncles. They even taped a picture of my twin sister to my incubator, which seemed to soothe me.

My family was finally able to welcome me home on a snowy March day, and my parents were thrilled to have both of their babies at home for the first time. Over the next several months, my parents learned the joys and challenges associated with caring for two newborns. Right from the start, my parents built a community around my sister and me, enlisting the help of friends and family. My mom and grandma Shelley would marvel at the rate that I seemed to be developing compared to my sister. I was the first to roll over, and when they stood me on their knees, I could push myself up. However, they would soon find out that my ability to push with my legs was a sign not of strength but of spasticity.

Because of the time I'd spent in the hospital, the doctors wanted to monitor my development and ordered testing once I reached five months. These tests led to a diagnosis of Extrapyramidal Cerebral Palsy and chronic drooling. This would set my family on the course of multiple doctors' appointments and several therapy sessions per week at the Shriners Hospital for Children in Portland.

As they struggled with the weight of having a disabled child and of being unsure about my future, my parents had to decide how they were going to raise my sister and me. Although they realized that I would require more assistance and attention as I grew, and that they were still unsure of what my abilities would be, they chose to raise me according to the same standards by which they raised my sister. Instead of giving up and enabling me, they were determined to help me reach my full potential, regardless of how difficult it was to see me struggle or how much time they had to spend transporting me to different appointments. Due to my parents' determination, I learned to never give up. In our house, the words "no" and "I can't" were not acceptable answers to the unique challenges I faced. At an early age I learned that as long as I tried and gave it my best effort, there would always be help available.

Throughout my life, I have revisited my first couple of years through self-reflection. Using the six links of turning bondage into tools of freedom, I've reflected on what lessons I learned in those early years and who the people were who saw me through them. Who helped me carry my chains? The most powerful lesson I learned during this time was that everybody has different types of challenges, so just because your challenges look much different, don't let it stop you. Don't take no for an answer!

I also learned that I can't be entirely independent. In all actuality, none of us are completely independent! We all need others to encourage us and lend a hand after we give it our best shot. Throughout my childhood, my family served as the starting point for what would become a powerful support system.

Reflection

At the end of each remaining chapter, I want to give you an opportunity to reflect on the lessons I have outlined in the chapter. I highly encourage you to keep a journal! Before writing this book, I wasn't keen on the idea of keeping a journal, due to the sheer fact of how long it takes me to type. However, I have recently found journaling to be freeing and insightful. If writing isn't your strong suit, try talking to a digital recorder. Get it out of your head! Meditate on your discoveries and revelations.

Sometimes you need to fight to survive! What were the events in my life that spawned the challenges that I've faced or am currently facing?

_____

_____

Has this event paralyzed me? Did I choose to fight? Am I still stuck? How so?

_____

_____

Change can only occur when someone decides to take action! What lessons did I learn from enduring this event or challenge?

_____

_____

How can I apply this to my life TODAY?

_____

_____

Who is encouraging me? If I need help, whom can I call?

_____

_____

Chapter 3: Free Falling

AS I MATURE BOTH IN age and in understanding of myself and the world we live in, I've become increasingly convinced that it is time for us to change our mindset and language regarding success and failure. I recently read a quote by former IBM president Thomas John Watson Sr. He states, *"If you want to increase your success rate double your failure rate."* While I wholeheartedly agree with this premise, I would recommend that we begin replacing the word failure with falling. In my experience, there is a very distinct difference between falling and failing.

Failing is a result of an attitude problem. There have been times in my life where I have felt like I had failed at something, most notably several psychology exams during my undergraduate studies. I've found that having an attitude of failure or defeat doesn't propel us toward our goals; rather, it adds more chains to hold us back. A synonym of failure is fault, which I find incredibly accurate. Whenever I've had an attitude of failure, my first tendency was to place blame on myself or others for not achieving my desired outcome. The attitude of failure can lead to self-pity, which ultimately leads to self-destruction. Self-pity is like a dense fog that prevents us from moving toward our achievements and looking for lessons in our past.

On the hand, falling cultivates an attitude of learning. It holds a lighter connotation than failing. Think of how we teach children to walk. They take a few steps, fall, and we help them up and tell them to try again. This needs to be our attitude in approaching our own shortcomings. Imagine if when your toddler fell your reaction was "You suck at walking! Why do you even try? You're never going to walk so just keep crawling!" This sounds outrageous, but it's what we say to ourselves when we fail. When we fall, it provides us with an opportunity to see the six links in action. We are able to self-reflect on questions such as "what did I trip on?"; "what was I doing well?"; and "who can help me up?"

Throughout my life, I have been no stranger to falling, both figuratively and literally. As with many people who have lifelong disabilities, my early childhood was filled with several types of therapies multiple times per week. My biggest goal in these therapy sessions was to become as mobile as possible. For me, I knew that meant that I needed to learn how to walk. Unlike most able-bodied kids, the process of learning to walk, without any mobility devices, lasted long into my grade school years. The length of this process granted me the opportunity to gain more experience with falling.

Although I fell many times in my younger years, one particular event still comes to mind. As a result of the progress I was making in physical therapy, I began to walk around the house independently nearing the end of first grade. One day after school I was walking down the hallway while talking to my younger sister, Becca, who was three at the time. As I approached the end of the hall, I lost my balance and fell backward, catching the corner of the wall. I immediately grabbed the back of my head and realized that I had a little more than a bump. When Becca and I saw that my hand was now covered in blood, she began to scream, which drew the attention of Brooke, my mom, and my grandma, who were in the basement. Because this was my first experience with stitches, it seemed like the whole family met us at the emergency room. As my dad and grandparents arrived, everyone was anxious to hear my perspective on the accident. Rather than blaming my sister or refusing to walk again, I simply told them that I shouldn't have been talking while I was walking.

This story, among others, taught me a valuable life lesson that extends far beyond learning how to walk. It taught me that falling is inevitable and that we have a choice in how we respond. On that day in the emergency room, I could have very easily developed an attitude of failure, placing fault on myself or others for the state that I found myself in, and decided to use my wheelchair. However, I chose to remember the progress I had made and looked for a lesson that could help me achieve my goal of walking independently. I learned that I didn't have enough competence in walking to multitask. Discovering this lesson also provide a new goal and motivation.

Although I learned to look for lessons in overcoming by literally falling, I have used these lessons from falling when attempting something new at school, in my transition from college into the workplace, even while I am writing this book. The inevitability of falling is relevant to any endeavor that you may embark on. Until you achieve your goals and become a master of what you are facing, you'll make mistakes and have some missteps. That's okay! The wonderful and exciting thing about falling is that we have the opportunity to learn more about ourselves and our mission and to better define our path to success. Everything begins with little steps. If you fall while taking a step, you haven't failed! Get up, learn from it, and try again!

In order for you to turn your bondage into tools of freedom, you must change your attitude and language when addressing your challenges. Are you feeling hopeless about being able to advance toward your goal? This is a sign that you're living with a failure mentality. Perform an attitude check! We do not fail! We advance toward our goals, and we will fall, but we'll learn, get back up, and try again! If you adopt this method as I have, you will not only feel better equipped for the future, but you'll begin to see a clear path to achieving your goals.

Reflection

In your journal or digital tape recorder, meditate on the following questions.

Do I have an attitude of failure? If not, when have I had an attitude of failure? What event(s) have sparked this attitude?

_____

_____

Change failing to falling and clear the fog of self-pity. What lessons can I glean from this fall?

_____

_____

Does this reveal any new goals or steps toward achieving my master goal?

_____

_____

Who can help me stand up and get back on the path? A family member? A friend? A mentor? A therapist?

_____

_____

What is one new step I'm going to take toward my goal? Be as specific as possible and include a timeframe. Remember, it just needs to be a small step!

_____

_____

Chapter 4: Find Your Uniqueness

As part of our human nature, we often find ourselves desiring to be exactly like another person. A certain level of this can be helpful in our pursuit of our goals. In our society, we refer to this as having positive role models. However, we must not lose sight of our individuality and the unique set of skills and talents that we inherently bring on our journeys. With self-reflection, we can find a healthy balance and map out the steps that lead to success.

Role models are key to our development, especially during our childhood. They provide us with a tangible image of the type of person we can become or what we can accomplish. Throughout my childhood, like most boys, I looked up to my father and wanted to be just like him. As I've grown into an adult, there have been different qualities in him that I have admired. Now that I'm an adult, it's his work ethic and his high value on family that I admire. However, in elementary school, I wanted to be like my dad because he played city-league baseball!

As a child with a severe physical disability, I was aware that I would probably never have the opportunity to play a team sport such as baseball. In fact, I had constant reminders, as I wasn't as mobile as my sisters or my classmates. Still, with the desire to play baseball, I turned my interest to learning everything I could about computers, which developed a strong bond between my uncle and me. However, my parents were committed to helping me find a way to play baseball and found a softball team for kids with disabilities called Challenger Little League. During the five years that I played, my dad and grandfather were involved with coaching the team. Through working with my coach, both on and off the field, I learned that I couldn't play like him, but I could do things that some of my teammates couldn't. We found my unique abilities and nurtured those skills. Eventually, I became the only player in our division to steal a base on cue.

This lesson also translated to my love of technology. Because of the fine motor skills it takes to manipulate peripherals, I've had to explore various assistive hardware and software to aid in my productivity and explore one of my passions. I view my unique setup with my assistive devices and in softball as growth opportunities. As I became more confident and competent with my system, I gained the skills to normalize my processes and advanced toward my goals. For example, when I started using a computer I used a giant joystick with an onscreen keyboard. Today, I'm writing this book using a regular keyboard and mouse, paired with predictive text software. The various alternative setups that I had enhanced my motor skills so I could reach my goal of working on any computer or tablet.

In order to reach our goals, we must find what makes us unique from our colleagues and role models, and embrace it. How do we find our unique abilities? I've found that most people, including myself, have difficulty discovering these abilities and talents because we are naturally in comparison mode. Comparison can become unhealthy and hinder self-reflection. We must stop comparing ourselves to others and start affirming ourselves!

Lately, I've had the pleasure of offering a workshop on positive affirmations to students in the Portland area, primarily in elementary schools. This workshop is an introduction to how self-reflection and encouragement from others help us build confidence and become the best versions of ourselves. I ask the students to give each other affirmations regarding their personalities or talents and skills. I begin there because often it's easier to see the uniqueness in our peers. Then I ask them to write an affirmation for themselves and have them keep both affirmations in a place where they can look at them when they're feeling discouraged.

The activities in this workshop are essentially the first and last link in the self-reflection process. As previously stated, the first link is the question of what.

Ask yourself:
What unique personality traits do I possess?
What are my gifts or talents?
What experiences give me a unique perspective?

The final link is who. Whom can you ask for feedback about what traits make you stand out from the crowd? Most of the time our peers and mentors can identify traits much more easily.

While positive affirmations seem so elementary, they are vital to our success. They help us enter into the process of turning our bondage into tools of freedom by ushering us in with a positive mindset. If we enter this process with a negative view of ourselves or unfair comparisons of ourselves to others, we won't be productive in developing a plan to achieve our goals and dreams! We are each uniquely qualified for our journey toward success. Find your uniqueness and develop it!

Reflection

In your journal or digital tape recorder, meditate on the following questions.

What unique personality traits do I possess?

_____

_____

What are my gifts or talents?

_____

_____

What experiences give me a unique perspective?

_____

_____

Whom can I ask for feedback about what traits make me stand out from the crowd?

_____

_____

Who is my role model?

_____

_____

Write yourself two positive affirmations and post them in a place that you'll see daily. This could on your office wall or bathroom mirror.

_____

_____

Chapter 5: Stand Up and Lead

ONE OF THE MOST MEMORABLE days of middle school was the day I fell on my face walking through the front doors. Let me set the scene.

It was early in my sixth-grade year, and I was beginning to establish a routine. Each morning my educational assistant would set up my walker and then help me walk down the stairs of the school bus. I would then begin my long trek to the sixth-grade wing, arriving at my homeroom class just before the bell rang. This was quite a workout for a kid who was used to an elementary half the size and didn't require the use of ramps. Nevertheless, I was adjusting

43

well to the new routine. However, on this particular morning, I happened to be a little more off balance than usual. Little did I know that it would be the cause of a chain of events that would last throughout the day.

As I entered the building, the wheels on my walker got caught on the threshold of the door and sent me toppling to the ground in a faceplant. Picture someone flipping over the handlebars of their bicycle, and that's essentially what happened to me, as I was enclosed by my walker from behind and from the sides, with handles out front. Sure, the fall didn't feel great and was slightly embarrassing, but I was used to falling. So I picked myself up and went about my day, almost forgetting what had happened.

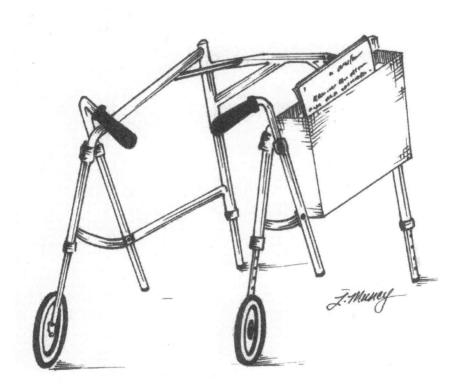

Several hours later, while I was in study hall, I received a note requesting my presence in the counseling office. Now, I wasn't an angel by any means, but I usually made sure that I stopped short of being sent to the office. That being said, I was confused and felt a bit anxious as I walked down to the office. When I walked in, I saw Brooke and a boy whom I had not yet met. I would soon learn about the altercation that had taken place after lunch. The boy had seemed to be mocking me by reenacting my fall for his friends. His biggest mistake was unknowingly exhibiting this behavior in the presence of my twin sister, who has always been very protective of me.

This incident bothered my sister much more than it did me. From a very early age, I subconsciously learned that often people let their ignorance get the best of them. Although I seemed to be unconcerned with the situation, it taught me a valuable life lesson that aided in breaking my chains to reach my full potential. I learned that everybody is known for something, and to some degree, we are in control of the image we portray. Through that experience, I realized that I had a choice to make. How do I want to be known? Do I want to be referred to as the disabled guy who falls frequently, or do I want to be recognized for something I would take pride in? I chose to develop myself as a leader by immersing myself in various leadership elective classes and eventually serving in student government. I decided that I wanted my peers and superiors to view me as a strong and capable person who provides unique insight.

How do you want to be known among your peers? What do you want your legacy to be? We are all faced with these questions throughout our lives. Unfortunately, we have a tendency to become so consumed by mediocrity and the mundane rhythm of life that we fail to take the time to ponder these life-altering questions. If we take

45

the time to reflect on how we want to be known, it changes our self-perception and changes our day-to-day actions. This is the "where" link in the process of turning bondage into the tools that lead us to succeed. Where do I want to be? Once we discover where we are going and who we want to be, it serves as motivation and often reveals the first steps we need to take to get there.

Not only has reflecting on these questions guided my past decisions, but I'm also continually asking myself where I want to be in my personal life, where I want to be in my professional life, and how I want to be known. One of my many practices I use while going through the six-link process is visualization. Several of my mentors have suggested this practice to me over the years. Through visualization, you are able to imagine the feeling of what you are pursuing, which creates a stronger bond. It's easier to keep in the forefront or your mind and gives you motivation when the journey seems impossible. Take, for instance, my decision to write this book, which I'll cover in length later in a future chapter. When I began the writing process over a year ago, I asked myself where I wanted to be and how I wanted to be known. I visualized myself speaking to a crowd about overcoming barriers, with a completed book in hand. This picture has helped me move past times of doubt and frustration regarding my ability to type at a reasonable pace.

By slowing down and comparing my current state with where I want to be, I position myself in such a way that I can set reasonable goals that help me progress. Often the goals I set and steps I discover are not giant leaps. They're baby steps, as simple as writing down two things I can do or research that day.

I wholeheartedly believe that if we all find time to self-reflect, especially on where we want to be or what we want to be known for, it would save us some frustration and boredom from spinning our wheels. If you're stuck and can't see where you're going, perhaps the first question is, what don't you want to be known for? Sometimes that question alone provides us with enough motivation to change our mindset and open our eyes to discover our purpose. This was how I found my passion for leadership. By being complacent and ignoring the opportunity to define where we want to be, we are risking being known for our shortcomings. Our challenges should not define us. I refuse to have my life dictated by mine. I have decided what I want to be known for and I continue to pursue it vigorously! Through self-reflection, you too can stand up, lead, and be known for your successes.

Reflection

In your journal or digital tape recorder, meditate on the following questions.

What challenges am I letting define me?

_____

_____

What do I want to be known for?

_____

_____

The experience with my peers and sister helped me realize what I didn't want to be known for. Sometimes the people who hold us down can help us identify the direction that we want to go in. Who can help me discover my purpose?

_____

_____

Visualize where you want to be. What does it look like? How does it feel? Make a copy of your visualization and keep it next to your positive affirmations.

_____

_____

Hey Friend, I hope you're enjoying the book so far, finding it both inspiring and empowering.

I have a favor to ask you. Would you consider giving it a rating on Amazon or Goodreads, please?

My mission is to help as many people as possible break their chains and achieve success. Your review will help others discover this book and begin their journey toward freedom and success.

To your dreams and success,

Chapter 6: Find Out Who Your Friends Are

IN THE PREVIOUS CHAPTER, I posed the question of what you want to be known for. In that context, I was exploring the idea of defining what we want our reputation to be and what we want others to recognize us for. This helps us create a vision for where we want to be and enables us to set the goals that will guide us to achievement. Although this is important, it's vital to look at this idea of being known through another lens. I think there is another pertinent question that revolves around being known. The question of am I known? Your response to this question will alter your ability to break free from your chains.

If you ask most people who knew me in high school, they would say that I was very popular. Although many people knew my name and I knew theirs, I did not feel known. There is a distinct difference between being known and being popular. To be known is to have others take an interest in you as an individual and enter into a reciprocal relationship that is built on trust, respect, and understanding. This relationship provides us with people whom we can relate to and confide in, and who will encourage us to strive to be the best version of ourselves. These relationships come easy to some, while others, including myself, have to pursue this for years.

In recent years, I have begun to share about how isolated I felt during the first few years of high school. Much to the surprise of my family, my freshman and sophomore years were rough. During my transition from middle school into high school, I had lost two people who played an important role in my day-to-day support system. My educational assistant, who had been with me for eight years, decided not to follow me to high school, and Tony, my best friend since the third grade, transferred to a private school. Attempting to find a group of peers who knew me as more than just the guy on the scooter, I often would join in with the crowd that Brooke would have over on the weekends. Because Brooke and I wanted to create autonomy from one another, my presence sometimes caused tension between us. As a result of this, I once again turned to technology to fill my time and a void.

Although I didn't have many peers that I called close friends, I had a couple of educational assistants whom I could confide in, and who knew my desire to be in positions of leadership. With their encouragement, I decided to step deeper into leadership roles, which gave me the opportunity to meet new people. Through the people I met in leadership, I was invited to an event called Young Life club.

From the first time I walked into the Young Life club, I knew that I had found a group of people who wanted to know me beyond just a casual hello as we passed in the hallway. In Young Life, I found a support system of peers who genuinely cared about each other's well-being and built a foundation of friendship that has lasted long after high school. In fact, some of my closest friends today are from that group.

As someone who strives to be as independent as possible, I have come to realize that having peers whom you can relate to and can confide in is vital to not only our success but also our well-being. When I was younger, I would have said that it was important to be popular and agreed that most people knew who I was. However, I have found that popularity without an intimate circle of friends will lead to loneliness and self-destruction. Popularity is not entirely a negative asset. In fact, it's important for us to have a wide range of connections. This is evident in the rise of social media platforms and the rising billions coming online in the next few years. However, this type of popularity and connectivity does not provide the support we need to push forward toward our goals. We mustn't neglect the formation of our inner circles! This is the foundation of our support system. We need to find peers to come alongside us to offer support and encouragement.

Who is in your corner?

I like to use a boxing analogy when thinking about our support systems. So cue the *Rocky* music!

In boxing, at the end of each round, the boxer retreats to their corner for a minute of rest. In their corner, they have a trainer, an assistant trainer, and someone to tend to their injuries. These three people are charged with the task of educating, encouraging, and aiding the boxer so that they can return to the fight. I love this analogy because sometimes it feels like a boxing match when we're pursuing our goals, and we need to take breaks along the way to learn, be encouraged, and address our wounds. This is why it's necessary to establish a few friends who can pick us up and encourage us when our missteps feel like uppercuts.

Reflection

In your journal or digital tape recorder, meditate on the following questions.

Do I feel known?

_____

_____

How am I cultivating my inner circle?

_____

_____

What are three steps that I can take to invest in my inner circle?

_____

_____

Who is in my corner?

_____

_____

Who is my coach? This is your mentor.

_____

_____

Who is my assistant trainer and cutman? These are your encouragers.

_____

_____

Chapter 7: Defying Gravity

HAVE YOU EVER FELT LIKE you were trying to defy gravity? Unless you are outside the confines of our planet, it is almost impossible to defy the laws of gravity. Many times our obstacles seem so insurmountable that we feel as if we'll never accomplish our goals. This could be a result of our own attitude, the feelings of our support system, or, even worse, the misinterpreted intentions of individuals in our support system. However, when we are faced with these times of uncertainty and defeat, we have the opportunity to make decisions that will influence the outcome.

Although I have faced many uphill battles that seemed impossible, one in particular has had a profound impact on my worldview and my drive to consistently persevere. I will never forget

57

the day that my friends came up to me and asked me to join the track team. Now, in my senior year of high school, I had a very light class schedule and filled my time with student government, youth group at my church, Young Life, and spending every minute with my friends from club, many of whom were on our high school track team. Because we had built our relationship on trust and encouragement, I had shared my lifelong desire to be part of a competitive team sport. They responded with an overwhelming encouragement to join the track team. I was highly skeptical, to say the least, as I could barely walk a quarter of a mile and couldn't even keep a decent walking pace, let alone run. After days of encouragement, I finally agreed to talk with the coaching staff, many of whom had taught me in previous years. All of the coaches were immediately on board with the idea and began brainstorming ways that I could contribute and events in which I could participate. As I expressed my hesitation, they explained that track is both a team and an individual sport. They helped me understand that I could compete by improving my personal record each meet. At that point, I was sold!

However, there were other obstacles that I was about to face, other than the obvious physical challenges. By the time I decided to join the team, they had already been holding practice for a week and I needed a physical exam before I could do anything with the team. On top of that, I had to use a wheelchair-accessible bus to transport my scooter to and from school. Because my specialized transportation was provided by the school district, we would have to submit a request to accommodate after-school practices. So naturally when I presented this to my parents with such a short timeline for completion, it caused some stress and arguments.

Although my mom was just stressed about working out the details in such a short timeframe, I perceived it as not having her support. From my point of view, I believed that she was worried about my ability to compete or the possibility of injuring myself. This was not the case. However, I learned that it's easy to misinterpret another person's intentions, resulting in the creation of an alternate reality that can feel very real.

Now, I'm the type of person that has to be listening to music any time I'm alone, especially when I'm upset or discouraged. Music calms me but it also has a way of speaking to me while I'm reflecting. In my worldview, I believe that God speaks to my soul through lyrics. I enjoy most types of music, but growing up around singers, dancers, and actresses, I have gained an appreciation for musical theater. While I was struggling with the belief that my mom didn't support my pursuit of this dream, I heard "Defying Gravity" off my sister's *Wicked* soundtrack. At that moment a verse resonated with me and changed my attitude in how I approach certain challenges. The verse says, "I'm through accepting limits, because someone says they're so. Some things I cannot change, but till I try, I'll never know!" From that moment on, I've consciously operated from the standpoint of trying everything I want to achieve, accepting things that I can't change, and refusing to let others dictate what my limits are. Although this revelation was birthed out of a false reality, it has greatly influenced who I am today.

Far too often, we give up on our vision because of limits others place on us, or, even worse, limits that we place on ourselves due to the lack of belief. We must start believing in ourselves! The most important lesson my coaches taught me that year had nothing to do with athletic techniques. This lesson was about building character and determination. I learned that if I believe in myself and have the drive to work hard, I can accomplish what I set out to achieve. The lesson, paired with the revelation from the song, has changed how I self-reflect and set goals for my future.

Believing in yourself is a mindset you must embrace. Without this forward-thinking attitude, it's impossible to gain traction toward our dreams. A vision without believing you can achieve it reaps the same outcome as an attitude of failure. We ultimately lose our vision in fog because we are not in a position to see our next steps.

My coaches and inner circle gave me the confidence to defy gravity, both figuratively and literally. I ended up running the one-hundred-meter dash and improving my PR at every meet. As I practiced, I found myself becoming stronger and improving my balance, thus decreasing the amount of times gravity won!

I believe that we were meant to soar toward our goals. With a little belief and self-reflection, you too can defy gravity!

Reflection

In your journal or digital tape recorder, meditate on the following questions.

What is the vision or goal in my life that seems as impossible as defying gravity?

_____

_____

_____

_____

Do I believe that I can achieve this?

_____

_____

_____

_____

What limits am I putting on myself?

_____

_____

_____

_____

What limits are others placing on me? Are these limitations reality or perceived?

_____

_____

_____

_____

What affirmations can I use to change my mindset?

_____

_____

_____

_____

Chapter 8: Push Your Limits

THE LIMITS WE PLACE ON ourselves act as a barrier on the path to discovering our purpose, which ultimately hinders our growth. If we are truly committed to the pursuit of our full potential, we must be willing to push our limits. This can be a terrifying endeavor. However, true growth can only occur when we step out in faith and make a conscious effort to improve ourselves.

I have seen this played out through many facets of my life, but perhaps one of the most influential experiences was the last youth retreat I attended with my church's high school group. The summers following my sophomore and junior years had been filled with various retreats and Young Life camps. However, after my high school graduation, my summer was going to be fairly low-key, with the exception of the graduation trip to Hawaii that my parents had promised Brooke and me. For the first time in years, I wasn't signed up for any camps, as I had already hit the max camp attendance for our Young Life group and my church was only offering a houseboat retreat on Lake Shasta in Northern California. I had made up my mind earlier in the year that a week on a houseboat would be nearly impossible for me, between needing a flotation device in the water and needing to be carried over the rough terrain when we were on shore. However, a few of my youth leaders were adamant that I attend. Although I wasn't overly excited and had some major reservations, I decided to go because I had some friends attending and I knew from previous experience that my leaders would do everything they could to accommodate and include me.

The first couple days went just as I had anticipated. I was extremely uncomfortable due to the long ride in a school bus, which caused my back to tense up, and the fact that I was stuck on a boat. As I began to slip into the fog associated with self-pity, we took a hike to a waterfall that we could slide down. Determined to provide me with the same experience as my peers, leaders and friends alternated carrying me on their backs and lifting me up the waterfall. As a person of faith, I believe that God is at work in every situation we find ourselves in, and seeing their determination reminded me to seek out how this trip could improve me and my relationships.

As I began to look for life lessons, I decided to step out of the boat and try to wakeboard. This experience was very empowering and filled with many faceplants. In between my epic wipeouts, there were periods of a few seconds of riding the wakes. Nearing the end of my run, I noticed that the entire youth group was on the roof of the houseboat, watching my attempt to wakeboard and cheering. As

I heard their cheers, I had an overwhelming feeling that the experience wasn't just about my attempt to ride a wake. After taking the time to reflect on what had transpired, I realized I had a platform to encourage others and share my faith. I decided to share this realization with my leader, who asked me to share my journey with the whole group the following evening.

Until this point in my life, I had avoided speaking in front of large crowds. I was very self-conscious about my speech impediment and was concerned that others would not be able to understand me. Once again I was faced with the choice to step out of the boat metaphorically. Deciding to step out in faith, I agreed to share what I had learned that week and how it deepened my faith. As I stood there and saw the reaction of the leaders and students, my realization was confirmed.

I had found my life's purpose. I have been put on this planet to encourage others and help them to overcome challenges so that they can reach their full potential.

This retreat was a defining moment in my life, as it revealed the purpose that drives all of my decisions and motivates me both personally and professionally. The process of receiving this revelation taught me two very valuable lessons regarding overcoming challenges and the pursuit of success.

The first lesson is that we cannot move past the limits we place on ourselves without leaving our comfort zone. Actually, escaping our comfort zone is more accurate! Isn't it our fear of the unknown that is the greatest perpetrator of our barriers? We're so

often too worried about falling or what others will think, or, worse, about feeling temporarily uncomfortable. This stunts our growth! We must escape the comfort zone and become comfortable with being uncomfortable. Then, and only then, will we be in a position to see substantial growth.

By being willing to step out of my comfort zone on the houseboat retreat, I learned how valuable self-reflection is in discovering your purpose. This was the first time I began to consciously think about the six links outlined in this book. Taking time to reflect on the past, the present, and what you're feeling will reveal your direction. By stepping outside of our comfort zone, we are able to enter this time of reflection with a new perspective.

Picture this. You're hiking on a trail and you know that there is a beautiful scene at the end, but you're not sure what it entails. Right before you approach a clearing that will give you a glimpse of your reward, you put up a roadblock and refuse to walk a few more steps because you're afraid of what may lie ahead. So you sit there and complain about not being able to see where you are headed. Eventually, you decide to cross the roadblock and discover that the most beautiful thing you've ever seen is off in the distance.

Our comfort zone hinders our growth and our ability to see what's in the distance waiting for us. Dare to cross the barrier! Get out of the boat! You might be surprised to see what awaits you!

Reflection

In your journal or digital tape recorder, meditate on the following questions.

What are the barriers I'm putting up?

_____

_____

_____

What steps can I take to escape my comfort zone? Who can help me cross the barrier?

_____

_____

_____

If I am outside my comfort zone, what is this experience teaching me? How is this revealing my purpose?

_____

_____

_____

From where I stand now, what do I see my purpose as?

_____

_____

_____

Chapter 9: Speak Up

I BELIEVE THE FIRST EIGHTEEN years of my life were preparing me for success by helping me develop one fundamental skill: the skill of self-advocating. Many people fail to embrace this powerful tool for a multitude of reasons. However, the most common is that society tells us that we should be self-made and not burden others with our needs. If you haven't picked up on this already, one of the central themes of this book and my story is that it's impossible to be completely independent. We must recognize that we need help and be willing to accept help from others. In order to accept this help, we must learn how to speak up and ask for what we need.

Upon graduating high school, I decided to attend a community college near where I lived. While my ultimate goal was to attend a university, members of my support system recommended that I ease into this transition, as there were many changes and decisions that I needed to make. College was definitely a new experience for me. For the first time I didn't have anyone keeping track of where I was or what I was doing throughout the day. Public schools made sure that, as a person with a disability who needed an assistant, I was watched all day, with a few exceptions. During my senior year of high school, I had convinced my case manager to let me be independent during the periods when I didn't have class or when I was in Student Government. However, in college I was finally free.

This newfound freedom did not come without some harsh realities. As a young teenager one of my favorite movies was *Spiderman*. I would watch that movie several times a year. As I entered my first year of college I learned that a certain line from that movie was very applicable. "With great power comes great responsibility." Now that I wasn't being supervised by a case manager, I had the responsibility to make sure I had the help and accommodations I needed to be successful in school and my personal life. For the first time, I was charged with the task of finding my own assistant and transportation through state services instead of having it provided through the school. Moreover, when it came to arranging classroom accommodations, the school didn't care what my parents said; they needed to hear it from me. Of course I never lost the support of my parents, but they recognized the importance of letting me navigate my new reality independently. Instead of taking charge, they began to wait until I asked for their assistance. I had all of the power and responsibility over my success and over ensuring that I was receiving the help I needed.

As with any new endeavor, I needed to use my method of self-reflection to fully understand what my support system had previously provided me with, what I wanted to achieve, what challenges I could anticipate, and how I was going to overcome them. Out of this, I realized that my greatest need was to find an assistant who could help me with the physical tasks associated with homework and getting around the city. Knowing the state would pay for someone to help me a few hours a week but being unsure of how to go about filling the position, I decided to postpone it as long as possible. While state services assured me that they could help me find someone, I was determined to hire someone that I was already comfortable with. Fortunately, to my surprise, Stephanie, one of my friends from Young Life, and I had registered for the same introduction to college course that was offered a few weeks before our fall term began. As we caught up on our lives, she shared that she was looking for employment and I shared that I was looking for help. Not only was that the beginning of a wonderful two-year working relationship, we also became best friends and each other's closest advisors.

Oftentimes when we seek help from others, the experience ends up being mutually beneficial for both parties. I used to buy into the ideology set forth by society regarding the need for assistance: asking for help is a sign of weakness and incompetence. Through my experience, I can no longer subscribe to that blatant fallacy. It requires a great deal of strength and self-awareness to admit to ourselves and others that we need help. Asking for help not only shows our strength and helps us advance toward our goal, it provides tremendous growth opportunities for both individuals. It's impossible to enter into a relationship, especially one of mutual assistance, and not grow as a person or in experience.

Seeking help can be extremely difficult, let alone realizing the areas in which we need assistance. It takes strength and self-reflection. If we are going to overcome our obstacles, we must take the time to identify our shortcomings and trust that others will help us reconcile those areas. This realization is possible through the use of the six links, but then it's up to you to seek out assistance. Once again there is a choice to be made. *Are you going to keep ignoring a fact that is halting true growth or are you going to speak up?* I hope that you speak up! Try it. You might just be surprised what opportunities are presented through this simple action.

Reflection

In your journal or digital tape recorder, meditate on the following questions.

Am I afraid to speak up? Why do I feel this way?

_____

_____

_____

What are the areas in my vision in which I anticipate needing assistance?

_____

_____

_____

Whom can I ask for help? Is it a coach, an organization, or a member of my support system?

_____

_____

_____

Chapter 10: Critical Planning

MY DISABILITY HAS TAUGHT ME many lessons over the course of my journey. I've had to learn patience and how to self-advocate, among others. However, I think the most impactful lesson to my success has been in understanding how critical planning is to our achievement. Trust me, this is easier said than done! I think of planning more as an art form than as a scientific method. What I mean by this is that planning looks different in each scenario. Sometimes the whole plan comes together and it's as clear as day. Other times it requires you to take a leap of faith before the puzzle pieces begin to fall into place. Regardless of how the planning manifests itself, we must hold our plans with a certain sense of flexibility, as we cannot control everything. Then why should we bother taking time to plan, if we're not holding on to it as divine law written on stone tablets? Planning is critical because it gives us a framework to help us reach our goals.

Think of planning as a roadmap. In the last few years, the traffic in Portland has increased immensely and there is often construction in multiple sections of the city, which makes the congestion worse. Now when I have a meeting across town, I have to look at a map to pick the best route. Although that might look like the best route when I leave, there may be unexpected detours. However, if I don't take time to look at where I'm going and just hope that I get to where I want to be, I could very easily miss my destination by miles, or, worse, I could head in the opposite direction! Planning puts us on a course toward overcoming our obstacles and making success a reality.

Although I can think of countless examples of how planning has played a vital role in my success, I can recall two incredibly important but very different planning processes surrounding my time at George Fox University. This first planning process required me to take a leap before the puzzle pieces began to come together.

As I ended my first year at the community college, I had remembered the purpose that was revealed to me on the houseboat trip the year prior, which was to help others overcome their challenges, particularly high school students. Therefore, I decided to pursue this by transferring to a Christian university and studying youth ministries. As I began searching for schools, I immediately decided that it would be easiest to attend one of the three bible colleges surrounding my parents' house, which would allow me to continue living at home. However, as with most things in my life, I realized that the easiest thing isn't always the right thing for you to succeed. After talking with several of my mentors, I decided to apply to George Fox University, which was the top-ranked Christian university in the Pacific Northwest and an hour away from home.

Part of my decision to attend George Fox was that there were financial resources available that could share the burden of paying for that quality of education. Up until this point in my college education, the state of Oregon had been paying for my schooling through Vocational Rehabilitation. However, I had friends at George Fox who were part of this scholarship initiative called Act Six. This is a leadership scholarship for young adults who have a passion to serve their community after college. When my friends discovered that I wanted to transfer, they encouraged me to apply for this scholarship. Still very apprehensive about the logistics of attending a school where I would need to live on campus, I decided to proceed through the rigorous application process. Upon being accepted to the university and being awarded the scholarship, which at the time was a full ride, I received a call from my friend. He had talked to his roommates and they had decided to invite me to live with them, and that they would assist me. This phone call was the start of nine months of planning, which was crucial to meeting my daily needs and ensuring my academic success and relational success with my roommates and new assistants.

My years at George Fox were successful because of the planning that took place after I took a leap of faith and worked with the people I had in my inner circle. The first few months of applying and taking that leap were terrifying, but if I hadn't been willing to put myself out there, I would not have been in a position to plan and I would have missed out on many wonderful experiences. We'll talk more about stepping out into uncharted territory in the next chapter.

Although I knew it was important to continuously plan very early in my college career, I remember the first time I became consciously aware of it. Throughout college I remained heavily involved with Young Life as a volunteer leader, and was hired on in a student-staff role during my senior year to prepare me for a staff position upon graduating. I vividly recall a conversation with my academic advisor, who was also my student staff trainer, and knew that my goal was to become an area director. Knowing my physical limitations and having previously held that position in Young Life, he asked me how I was going to do this job. His intentions were not mean-spirited, as he wanted me to succeed and thrive after college. He simply knew the demands of the job and wanted me to prepare. From that conversation, he and some other longtime staff helped me to create a plan to help me enter the early days of my career with confidence and a sense of direction.

Although both of these stories include assistance from mentors and friends, planning is largely a discipline requiring self-reflection. I recall countless nights of lying awake, using the six links to formulate my next steps. The self-reflection aspect of the planning process is so important, as it gives us ownership over our actions and progress. Our inner circle and mentors are there to act as a sounding board and help us refine our steps. Ultimately we have to have ownership over our roadmaps. It not only provides us with a greater sense of accomplishment but also keeps us motivated, knowing that we are following our own agenda, not one that we're given.

Taking time to plan through self-reflection is more than a helpful life skill; it's a gift. If you take the time to be attentive in self-reflection and create a plan to achieve your goals, it'll save a lot of time and energy. As you reflect, think of your plan in terms of your favorite map app! You have an overview that shows a suggested route. This is great for defining your overall objective. Take a snapshot of it to refer to periodically, but don't live there! It's often overwhelming! Go to the turn-by-turn directions! It helps you stay focused and gives you the ability to clearly problem-solve when you're faced with a detour.

I encourage you to check your overview to remind you of where you're going and your rearview to remind you how far you've come, but live in the details. Focus on your next step. This planning and goal-setting process has opened many doors for me and I know these six links can do the same for you.

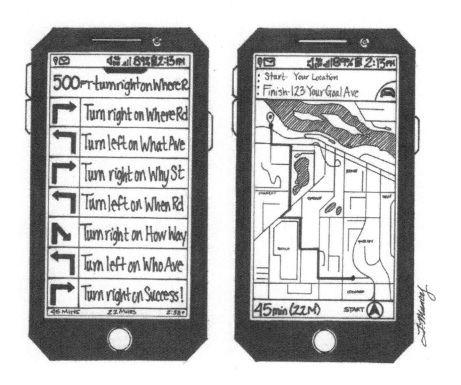

Reflection

In your journal or digital tape recorder, meditate on the following questions.

Where

Where do I want to be? Be as descriptive as possible. This is the overview version of your map. Refer back to this periodically to remind yourself of your desired end result.

_____

_____

What

What challenges, circumstances, or uncertainties have prevented me from taking steps toward achievement?

_____

_____

What barriers or detours do I anticipate running into?

_____

_____

Why

Why are these challenges, circumstances, or uncertainties preventing me from advancing toward my dreams?

_____

_____

Why am I anticipating these barriers or detours?

_____

_____

When

When do I want to arrive at my destination? It's very important to demonstrate flexibility with this deadline, as you will encounter detours and setbacks. As long as you are making progress, don't be ashamed to keep resetting deadlines.

_____

_____

How – Set goals for yourself. This is the details view. These questions can be reversed. I decided to order them like this because I tend to see the big picture first and work my way down to the steps I can take today.

How can I advance toward my dream this year?

_____

_____

How can I advance toward my dream this month?

_____

_____

How can I advance toward my dream this week?

_____

_____

How can I advance toward my dream today?

_____

_____

Who

Who can I talk to about my dream and goals? Find a mentor.

_____

_____

Will they ask me the tough questions?

_____

_____

Will they keep me accountable to making progress or to the deadlines that I set?

_____

_____

Who are the people in my inner circle that will provide honesty and encouragement?

_____

_____

Chapter 11: Uncharted Territory

HAVE YOU EVER FELT A strong calling or pull toward a dream but have equally strong reservations due to past experiences, inadequacies, and uncertainties? I'm confident that most, if not all of us, have felt this tension at one point in our journey. I have experienced this tension throughout my entire life. In fact, I have felt this in many of the stories that I've included in the previous chapters. Through these experiences, I have found that tension is a natural part of overcoming adversity and pushing forward toward our goals. Not only is it a normal part of growth, but tension also creates a healthy level of discomfort. How can feeling uncomfortable be healthy? I know that this sounds crazy, but before you skip this section, let's take some time to unpack this idea. Having an understanding of this will help in our discussion about uncharted territories.

As we face uncertainties and our feelings of inadequacies, we often become uncomfortable with our current situation. This is healthy because feeling uncomfortable requires a response. When we're feeling uncomfortable, we must take action, whether that means removing ourselves from a situation, changing our behavior, or simply getting off our rear ends. In my life, I have two daily reminders of how being uncomfortable requires us to do something. The first is the condition of my body. It's common knowledge that Cerebral Palsy is not a progressive condition. It's neither curable nor does it get worse over time. However, I have realized that as I get older it has become increasingly important for me to keep active so that my muscles don't stiffen too much. So as much as I enjoy lying in my bed and binge-watching Netflix on the weekends, I know that once my body starts feeling uncomfortable, I'd better get up and move.

My other reminder is the courtesy of my best pal and one of the greatest gifts I've ever received, my service dog Stanley. I may be a little biased, but I'm pretty sure that Stanley is the best dog ever! As near perfect as Stanley is, I still need to use his corrective collar from time to time. When I received Stanley this past summer, I was required to attend a two-week training so I could learn how to effectively work with him. As an animal lover, I was initially concerned about using corrections. However, I learned that the collar doesn't hurt them but rather makes them uncomfortable so that they will change their behavior. I think that we can look at the unsettling feeling that accompanies our insecurities and uncertainties as a form of correction to help us gain the right mindset and attitude.

I have found that I have felt the most uncomfortable, in regards to overcoming challenges and pursuing dreams, when I'm faced with entering uncharted territory. I define uncharted territories as opportunities that you have little to no experience in or as building something from the ground up. Both components of this definition can be equally intimidating and terrifying; however, we must not be afraid of the unknown. The fear of the unknown or of being inadequate is similar to having an attitude of failure. The fog of self-pity rolls in, and we become paralyzed. This may sound harsh, but I don't believe that any of us are perfectly skilled to reach our dreams when we begin our assent. By working through our adversities and being attentive in our self-reflection, we gain the skills we need over time. Therefore, we should acknowledge our insecurities and uncertainties but continue to push toward our dreams. Who knows, your inadequacies might end up being some of your greatest strengths.

This definition of uncharted territory has been the perfect way to describe my professional career up until this point. Before I entered my second year at George Fox University, I interviewed for a student-staff position with Young Life for the first time, which I was not chosen for due to my level of involvement. Although I was disappointed, it was the right decision, and it gave me a year to gain more experience. As I met with Aaron, the area director for Newberg, early in the school year, we talked about what I needed to achieve in order to justify being a paid intern. It was determined that I needed to take ownership over a ministry, which was the same requirement for my peers. Now, Aaron had wanted to start up a Capernaum club, which is Young Life's ministry to teens and young adults with disabilities. With the desire of helping me become an intern the following year, he asked me if I would help him start it by taking ownership of it. My response was "Hell no!" I know that sounds awful, but I explained to him that since middle school I had tried to separate myself from the disability community out of fear that people would assume that I had an intellectual disability.

Although we ended our meeting with the agreement that we would explore other options, the idea of starting a Capernaum club kept me awake at night for multiple weeks. Regardless of my insecurities and uncertainties, I had an overwhelming feeling that this was the next step in my journey. Not knowing what the future would hold, I approached Aaron and said, "I don't know what I'm doing but let's start the planning process!" One of the first steps we took was to visit an existing club in a neighboring town. The visit to that club changed my attitude toward people who have disabilities, and I fell in love with the ministry.

That first year of implementing the new Capernaum taught me the most about dealing with being uncomfortable. In Young Life Capernaum, we have a saying: "Be comfortable with being uncomfortable." This means that when you serve kids with disabilities, you're bound to be in an uncomfortable situation, and that's okay. If you spend time with a kid who drools, you'll probably be drooled on. Heck, if you're a leader in my Capernaum club, the team leader has probably drooled on you! Although I love what that saying means, it went much deeper for me. Not only did I have to become comfortable with caring for kids with disabilities, but I also had to become comfortable with my insecurities. Although the tension of my calling and insecurities drove me to take action, my insecurities didn't vanish overnight. I continuously had to be attentive through self-reflection and identify them so that they couldn't take control over me and my journey.

After implementing Newberg Capernaum as the team leader and intern for two years, I had that desire to start a Capernaum club in Portland upon graduating with my bachelor's degree. As I began talking with the regional director for Oregon, it became apparent that if I were to start this ministry, it was going to look quite a bit different. In Newberg, we had been supported by the community established by the twenty years of Young Life in that town. Due to unforeseen circumstances, the area in Portland was unable to provide the same support. However, the regional director believed in me and allowed me to start a Capernaum area. By default, I had become acting area director right out of college, a position I had been dreaming about since my first year in community college. Although I was excited to take on this new challenge, I was a little overwhelmed by the task at hand. Because I had made such a compelling case in the interview along with the two-year plan I had written, we decided to diverge from the protocol of gaining community support before selecting the staff person. Therefore, I was charged with the task of finding community support as well as financial support and leaders. Although I had support and supervision from the organization, it often felt like starting a new philanthropic business.

I have been in the role of acting area director for almost five years. There have been many highs and lows along way, as well as many lessons. If this job has taught me anything about how to navigate uncharted territory, it is that confidence is key in your ability to make progress. Confidence is our shield against allowing our insecurities to control our mind, attitude, and progress. This confidence is an inward and outward belief in ourselves that we have the determination to take the next step toward success. I love the saying "fake it till you make it" in regards to exuding confidence. Oftentimes when we are in uncharted territory, our lack of confidence hinders our ability to follow through with the goals that we set forth for ourselves. Am I saying that we should boast and force ourselves to believe that everything we do or touch will turn out solid gold? Of course not; that would be foolish! What I'm saying is that it's important to be confident in yourself and your self-awareness, so that you can follow through with the steps in your plan. For example, in my first year of directing the Capernaum area, I had no clue what I was doing the majority of the time; however, I was confident in my vision, as well as my gifts and shortcomings. Not only did this confidence allow me to push myself but it also attracted others to the vision and the cause. Once other people surrounded the mission, the confidence in my shortcomings allowed me to ask for help in those areas without any reservations.

In previous chapters, we have talked about the importance of positive affirmations. In my workshop on this topic, I explain to the students how one positive affirmation from a peer, or even yourself, can have a long-lasting impact on your confidence. I give the example of how I got involved with the track team in high school and how that encouragement from my friends has stayed with me through every time of uncertainty and feeling of inadequacy that I've faced. These affirmations are crucial to fostering a belief in ourselves that gives way to feeling confident.

We'll talk more about the importance of surrounding yourself with people who believe in you in the next chapter. As we close this topic of launching into uncharted territories, I want to leave you with some encouragement. Don't let the fear of uncertainty or inadequacy paralyze you and prevent from pursuing solutions to your adversities or entering uncharted territory. We cannot remain stagnant. You are unique, and you have ideas, strengths, and weaknesses that the world needs to see! Take time to reflect, identify your strengths and shortcomings, and plan out your steps. Be confident, give in to the tension, and take action. Then brace yourself for one very fulfilling and wild ride!

Reflection

In your journal or digital tape recorder, meditate on the following questions.

Is there any tension that I'm feeling due to uncertainties and insecurities?

_____

_____

What are the insecurities or uncertainties that I'm facing in regards to overcoming my challenges and reaching my goals?

_____

_____

What actions is this tension prompting me to take? Set time-sensitive goals.

_____

_____

What uncharted territory am I facing?

_____

_____

In which ways can I exude confidence?

_____

_____

Who is helping me build confidence through encouragement? Write down their encouraging words, so that you can remember them when you feel discouraged.

_____

_____

Revisit the positive affirmation that you wrote at the end of chapter 4. Write it again, and then read it aloud. This helps you own the affirmation!

_____

_____

Chapter 12: Believe

RECENTLY, AS I WAS PREPARING to teach the second half of my positive-affirmations workshop in my friend's fourth-grade classroom, one of her colleagues introduced me to a YouTube clip of Dr. Maya Angelou from her appearance on Oprah's Master Class in 2011. This short clip was simply titled "Be a Rainbow in Someone Else's Cloud." Although this was just a brief snippet of the interview, it was filled with excellent insight regarding diversity and the importance of being kind to one another. As I reflected on this video, one quote, in particular, stood out to me. Dr. Angelou stated, "and one of the things I do when I step up on a stage, when I stand up to translate, when I go to teach my classes, when I go to direct a movie, I bring everyone who has ever been kind to me with me. Black, white,

Asian, Spanish-speaking, Native American, gay, straight, everybody. I say, come with me, I'm going on the stage. Come with me; I need you now." This quote reminds me of the important role other people play in building our self-confidence and how they contribute to our success. As I stated in previous chapters, those in our inner circle often have an easier time identifying our potential and qualities in ourselves than we do. When we choose to listen to our encouragers, embracing those qualities and living up to our full potential, we carry those individuals with us into our next endeavor. I have witnessed this time and again in my life, especially over the last several years.

Perhaps the greatest example of this concept is the item you're holding or what you are reading on your electronic device. Yes, this book is a tangible example of how my inner circle helped me gain confidence in myself by encouraging me to live up to the potential and qualities that they saw in me. Since my high school days, people have told me that I needed to write a book. Because of my writing style and unique outlook on life, many of my assistants consistently encouraged me to explore the idea of writing a book, or at the very least consider a career in journalism. Up until several years ago, I shrugged this off as an amusing idea, but I was not convinced that I had the stamina to produce a book, let alone anything of value to offer readers.

As I began the Capernaum ministry in Portland, I invited some family and friends to join in this philanthropic endeavor. Over the course of two years, one of these friends, Allan Wich, soon became my personal and professional mentor. As a person who has made his career mission to help other entrepreneurs, Allan saw the potential in me to achieve more than I believed I could. For years, as we met to discuss plans for the ministry, he would always bring up that I was doing a great job running our Capernaum area, but he saw potential in me to impact a global audience through writing, speaking, coaching, and teaching. Being only a few years into my career, I was confident that I was in the position that I was supposed to be in. However, I respect his opinion as a friend and professional, so I would indulge in conversations and make mental notes of the affirmations he gave me. This was a monthly occurrence until one day I woke up and felt the tension. It wasn't that I wanted to abandon the career that I had built; it was a feeling of being unsatisfied and stuck. I had just spent three years working my way up to a full-time position, and due to lack of financial growth, I was facing being "laid off" for nine months and returning as a part-time employee. As reality sank in, I realized that I loved my job, but I had a unique story and outlook on life that could be valuable for a larger population than just a small Capernaum club on the east side of Portland. This is exactly what Allan had been encouraging me with; I just needed to arrive at a place where I could accept it as truth. This tension drove me to take action by learning from my active and silent mentors, which helped me accept that holding a full-time position with my current job wasn't going to be a life-giving option for me.

Active and silent mentors are the people who have gone before us, pursuing similar goals or conquering similar challenges, and have found a certain level of success. Although both types of mentors are important, they have a distinct difference. Active mentors are those that we have an ongoing personal relationship with, whereas silent mentors are individuals that we follow through books, social media, conferences; perhaps we have met them or corresponded with them a few times but don't have permanent face-to-face access to them. To see a complete list of my active and silent mentors, please visit my website.

As I consulted with my inner circle and mentors, I realized, and in some ways was reminded, that my passion was speaking to groups and working with people in a one-on-one setting. This led me to study how my silent mentors achieved success in speaking and coaching, and I found a common denominator, which was that they all had authored a book! It's interesting that my passion had once been my greatest insecurity, speaking, and that the path to achievement led me to confront one of my biggest doubts, authorship. I'll touch on speaking later in this chapter. However, I'd like to continue to address the process of writing this book and why it's so reflective of Dr. Angelou's quote.

As soon as I realized that I should write this book, in order to more effectively help people to break their chains by overcome challenges and reaching their full potential, I began a writing process that has lasted over two years. The first year consisted of creating multiple concepts and outlines for the basis of this book. I chose this one because this self-reflection has the central point of everything I've overcome and accomplished, besides my faith, and I believe it will help the most people. However, the rejected concepts could appear in future projects. After a year, I had a complete concept and detailed outline, so my mentor suggested that I sign up for a crowdsourcing service called Publishizer, which helps authors gain support and attract publishing companies. As my campaign gained momentum, I began to type, and as I began to type paragraph after paragraph, my insecurities came flooding back. "You can't do this! It's two a.m., you've been typing since seven p.m. and have written under a thousand words. What makes you think people are going to want to read this? It's too short to be a REAL book! God, my back hurts SO BAD! Why are you torturing yourself? GIVE. IT. UP. MAN!"

I have wanted to throw in the towel on this project so many times this past year. Between late nights of what seemed like minute progress, back pain that lasted for weeks, trying to muster up enough energy to fight through the pain and spasticity to complete the next chapter, and missed deadlines, I was ready to give up or ask someone to take my outline and write the rest for me. Then I would return to the six links of turning my bondage into tools of freedom, and it would remind me why I was writing this. The process would help me set new deadlines as I was reminded that I had little control over the tightness of my muscles, so I had to be flexible and take the time to recover. As I reflected on the question of who, I thought of my family and friends in my inner circle, my mentors, all of the Publishizer backers, and you, the reader, and I realized that I am not alone! Every late night, you were with me, cheering me on to the finish line. In a sense, every time I sat down to type I was saying, "Everybody come with me, I'm typing! Come with me; I need you now!"

This process would also remind me why I refused to dictate or allow someone to ghostwrite this book. One of the central themes of this book is how to show perseverance in the face of adversity. In fact, one of my taglines is "encouraging an attitude of perseverance and inclusion." What kind of example would I be setting if I didn't write my first book on my own? I was reminded of another reason as I was watching a football game the other day. A line from a certain adult beverage commercial summed it up perfectly. The ad said, "the tougher the climb, the sweeter the reward!" By not taking sole ownership of this book, not only would I be doing you a disservice, but I would also be diminishing my sense of accomplishment.

Dr. Angelou's concept is also apparent in the discovery of my passion for speaking. Through my friends' and mentors' encouragement, I realized that I have a unique story and valuable lessons to share. Because of this, I began speaking and consulting with a number of business, schools, and churches. As I was put into positions to refine my craft, my insecurities began to disappear. This doesn't necessarily mean my speech impediment improved, although I have implemented techniques to make myself more understandable; rather, it means I have more confidence when I stand in front of a crowd. I don't stand there alone. I stand there with everyone who believes in my ability to help others!

Before deepening my relationship with my mentor, I would have never dreamed of writing a book, being a keynote speaker, hosting a podcast, or even teaching in an elementary school classroom. I didn't see my potential or the unique qualities and insights I've been given. Once I started believing in myself and that I had valuable information that could help people, it unlocked various rewards and opportunities. Due to this belief system, I am beaming with anticipation of what the future holds for me. It is my desire that you also feel this sense of belief and hope!

My encouragement to you is to link up! Find a mentor! This process of finding a mentor who can encourage you to reach your full potential is vital to your success. Sometimes the strength of pulling ourselves up the mountain is not enough; we need to link up with someone who is further along than we are. As you are looking for someone to link up with, don't forget to look down and lend a hand. There is always someone behind you who needs to learn from your experience. Please don't miss your opportunity to be a rainbow in someone's clouds!

Reflection

In your journal or digital tape recorder, meditate on the following questions.

What are my current clouds?

_____

_____

What insecurities are in these clouds?

_____

_____

Whom do I bring with me when I'm facing these insecurities?

_____

_____

Who are my silent mentors? Why do I follow them?

_____

_____

What can I learn from watching their experiences?

_____

_____

Is there someone that I should be following? Ask your inner circle and mentor to recommend a coaching program, book, or someone they follow you could learn from.

_____

_____

Whom can I link up with?

_____

_____

Who are my active mentors? Do they see potential in me that I have yet to take ownership of? Will they ask me the tough questions?

_____

_____

Who is linked up to me? How can I be an encouragement to them? Be a rainbow in someone's clouds!

_____

_____

Chapter 13: Be Attentive

Being attentive may be the most difficult trait for our society to maintain. We live in an environment where technology allows us to access virtually everything with a touch or a click. As amazing and useful as this technology is, it has an adverse effect on our patience and attention span. The problem here is two-fold. Because we have instant access to almost any piece of information, we want it short, sweet, and to the point, and we want it yesterday! The second part of the problem is that we're always connected, so we're bombarded with information. Most of the time the information is useless to us, so we're always half listening for information that pertains to our situation and sifting through it to pick out the golden nuggets. This has significantly damaged our ability to be attentive in our interpersonal relationships, and, I would be willing to argue, with ourselves.

Perhaps my biggest frustration with my disability is my speech impediment. Sure, my spastic muscles can be a real pain in the ass at times, but I have come to accept that I need help with certain tasks. However, the clarity of my speech depends on me and the listener. Although I would give anything to not deal with communication obstacles, I have come to view it as both a curse and a blessing. How can having a speech impediment be a blessing? These challenges demand that others stop everything and give their undivided attention in order to fully grasp my message. I have heard this time and again; however, these two examples from the last several years come to mind.

Several years ago while I was just establishing the Capernaum ministry and I was in between personal assistants, I met a young lady named Madison who wanted to be a leader. A mutual friend had arranged the meeting and came for the first part to aid in the introductions. Our friend was only able to stay for a few minutes and, not having an assistant, we found ourselves in the coffee shop talking as best we could. Over the years, Madison and I have become great friends, and regularly catch up over coffee when she's home from college. Last year as we met at our usual Starbucks, she said, "Blake, you know what you've taught me? You've taught me how to listen!" She went on to explain that during our first meeting, she could not understand my speech at all, but over the years she realized that when she was focused solely on what I was saying, my speech was very understandable.

A few weeks ago, I unintentionally conducted a social experiment. I call it unintentional because I was merely asking for feedback from my social media followers, but the results were fascinating. In 2015, I began the Breaking Chains Blog, which morphed over time into a video blog and podcast. After a brief hiatus to work on this book, I decided to make an update episode to let people know that I was still around and give them an update on what I was working on. Plus, I really wanted to test the new microphone that I had received for Christmas. During the hiatus, I made the switch to a more streamlined podcast-hosting platform so I would not have so many steps to get it on to the iTunes Store. However, I realized that I could only upload an audio file, due to storage limitations. As I uploaded the audio file, I decided to not put subtitles on the video that I would soon post to Facebook, saving me at least four hours of production time. If iTunes users didn't receive that luxury, why should Facebook's? On a whim, as I posted the video on my page, I commented: "Could some of you message me with what percentage of my speech was understandable and if there's anything that would help you understand my speech better?" The responses poured in from listeners ranging from people I've never met to people who had been around me a few times to good friends. Understandably, my good friends could understand me but wanted the subtitles back. The individuals who had been around me a few times couldn't understand my speech and wanted subtitles. However, much to my surprise, all of the comments from the people that I don't know personally said that they understood everything perfectly.

This spontaneous poll prompted many discussions within my inner circle regarding the lack of attentiveness in our relationships. The fact is that when something is new or if we believe something is of value, we give a little more effort to give our undivided attention. As I reflected on the lack of attention we give in our external communications, I began to wonder if we do the same with our internal communication. Are we taking the time to listen to our hopes and dreams, or to clear our minds so that we can effectively self-reflect? After looking at the periods when I used the six links, I realized that I had to make a conscious effort to sit down and listen to where my heart and mind were leading. I learned that my mind is distracted with the information that bombards us, and I'm confident that my experience with this is not an abnormality. We must learn to be present and attentive in our reflections on a daily basis.

How can we be present in our reflections when the world around us won't be quiet? I have struggled with this question for a long time, and I have found the answer in prayer and meditation programs. Wait, stay with me. I'm not going to get "churchy" on you. Although I pray quite a bit, I also use meditation when I'm overwhelmed. When I pray and meditate, I feel like my brain is the Indianapolis Raceway! Thought after thought racing by, disrupting what is supposed to be a relaxing moment. Every expert I have listened to suggested acknowledging the thought, then letting go and refocusing. I have found that this principle is also useful while reflecting on the six links. I suggest when you're flooded with thoughts, pull out another piece of paper, then make two columns titled "Save for Later" and "Throw Away." Write down the unrelated but helpful thoughts under "save for later" and the rest under "throw away," then turn your attention back to your current link. This physical action helps you remove the thoughts from your mind so that you can clearly reflect and set goals for your success.

Closing Remarks

As I sat and wrote this book, I had an opportunity to reflect on key periods in my life. Throughout this process I was able to see how I used the six links of turning bondage into tools of freedom and the impact it's having on my journey toward success. The first step of turning bondage into tools of freedom is choosing to enter a time of self-reflection. The tension between where you are and where you want to be is too great! Take action! Go back to your earliest memory of the challenges you face and use this process. I guarantee that you will learn something about that chain and that you can use as a tool today to help you get to where you want to be. Once you have reflected on where you've been and what chains you have in your toolbox, go for it! Don't be afraid of falling! Discover your purpose! Make a plan! Gather your inner circle and mentors! Be attentive! Chase your dream, pull yourself up that mountain! Most importantly, don't take no for an answer!

Reflection

In your journal or digital tape recorder, meditate on the following questions.

Do I have trouble with being attentive? Why?

_____

_____

What can I do to be more attentive in my external communication? (People you interact with)

_____

_____

What can I do to be more attentive in my internal communication? (Your self-awareness during your time of reflection)

_____

_____

Where do I want to be? Be detailed.

_____

_____

How can I advance toward my success today? Set a goal.

_____

_____

Who is in my inner circle? Who are my active and silent mentors?

_____

_____

Whom can I share my story and experience with? Be a rainbow in someone's clouds!

_____

_____

What are one or two concepts I learned from this book that I'm going to apply in my life?

_____

_____

More from Blake

Blake has created a *FREE* online companion course with multimedia content and additional resources. For more information, please visit www.breakingchainsbooks.com.

Blake is also available to speak at your events! For booking information, please visit www.blakeshelley.com.

Want to connect with Blake? He would love to hear from you!

Blake B. Shelley International

PO Box 195

Fairview, OR 97024

Blake@BlakeShelley.com

(347) 690-5154

Acknowledgments

A SPECIAL THANK-YOU to my backers on Publishizer and everyone who contributed their time and talents to this project! Your support is invaluable, and I could not have seen this through to fruition without you.

Linda Adalsteinsson
Madison Adrian
Ed and Traci Allen
Brianne Alley
Jennifer Babcock
Tim and Monica Brunner
Donald and Marylou Compton
Andy and Krystle Coombes
Christopher Cumby
Mary Jane Erwin
Jessi Freitag
Anna Gray
Randy and Stacy Hamar
Cierra Hayes
Damian and Annalise Hume
Jeremy Lloyd
Tony Muncy

Steve and Becky Paulson

Wes Poirier

Dave and Jen Proehl

Aaron Rauch

Marilyn Redwine

Sharon Scheurer

Stephanie Sequeira

Karen Shannon

Michael and Rhonda Shepard

Kyle and Lydia Shepard-Kiser

Fischer Stewart

Allan and Mary Ellen Wich

Katie Wich

About the Author

As a person with a disability, Blake has had to overcome many obstacles and challenges over the course of his life. At the age of six months, Blake was diagnosed with Cerebral Palsy (CP), which was due to a lack of oxygen at birth. The Mayo Clinic defines Cerebral Palsy as a disorder of movement, muscle tone, or posture that is caused by an insult to the immature, developing brain, most often before birth.

CP has made everyday tasks (ADLs) such as eating, walking, and typing extremely difficult. However, it has also taught him how to persevere while not being defined by a disability. It was ingrained in Blake by his parents and support system to never give up on his goals.

The confidence Blake found through his faith, family, and friends enabled him to attend George Fox University in Newberg, OR, on a scholarship through the Act Six Leadership Initiative (founded by Northwest Leadership Foundation and the Portland Leadership Foundation), and earn a Bachelor of Arts degree in Christian Ministries.

Since graduating from George Fox, Blake has devoted his time and resources to improving the quality of life of others, particularly those who have been impacted by disability, as well as educating the public about physical and emotional hurdles faced by young entrepreneurs. He has pursued this through promoting disability awareness in public schools, mentorship, disabilities advocacy, disabilities ministries, and educating the general public through speaking engagements. Using these experiences as a foundation, Blake is now bringing his message of breaking chains to those seeking success in their personal and professional lives.

Additional Resources

For more books and journals in the Breaking Chains series, please visit **www.breakingchainsbooks.com**

Education Edition

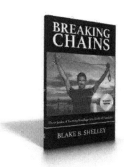

Business Edition

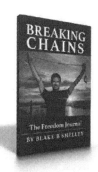

The Freedom Journal

99 Motivational Quotes to Break Your Chains

Made in the USA
Lexington, KY
27 November 2019